ENDURING
years

A Migrant Cotton Picker's Memoir

DR. GLORIA GRIFFIN, EDITOR

iUniverse LLC
Bloomington

ENDURING YEARS
A MIGRANT COTTON PICKER'S MEMOIR

Westview Publication, Southwestern Oklahoma State University, holds the copyright for any materials used in Enduring Years: A Migrant Cotton Picker's Memoir that corresponds directly with the essay, "Enduring Years," printed in the Westview spring 1982 issue.

iUniverse books may be ordered through booksellers or by contacting:

iUniverse
1663 Liberty Drive
Bloomington, IN 47403
www.iuniverse.com
1-800-Authors (1-800-288-4677)

ISBN: 978-1-4917-3092-8 (sc)
ISBN: 978-1-4917-3095-9 (e)

Library of Congress Control Number: 2014906894

Printed in the United States of America.

iUniverse rev. date: 05/30/2014

ENDURING
years

Contents

Foreword.. vii

Preface.. ix

Acknowledgments... xi

Introduction.. 1

Grandfather: Handing History to the Next Generation.............. 5

Father and Son: Rolling Stones.. 9

Billie and Ella: Vigilance and Strength....................................... 17

Family: Full House.. 27

Resilience: The Struggle Continues... 59

Endurance: Glory in Tribulation... 67

References... 75

About the Author... 81

Foreword

Many survivors of the Tulsa Race Riot of 1921, including my grandparents, did not talk about it. With an incredible amount of courage, tenacity, and faith, they silently endured. In the same way, entire subcultures of African American sharecroppers were able to weather the harshest conditions since the end of slavery and to carve out a sustainable life and a promise of a better future for their children. *Enduring Years: A Migrant Cotton Picker's Memoir* gives us a rare look into the life of a sharecropper named Billie Griffin. His memoir picks up where slave narratives of Oklahoma left off.[1] He filled in the blank spot between the Oklahoma stories about the urban entrepreneurs of Deep Deuce in Oklahoma City, the success of Black Wall Street in Tulsa's Greenwood district, and the early agricultural success of Oklahoma's all-black towns.

Griffin's memoir dredged up a faint memory of my father telling me that he was born in a cotton field in Grandfield, Tillman County, in southwest Oklahoma. He also told of the family lining the base board with two-by-four planks and sleeping on the floor to guard against gunfire from Ku Klux Klan night attacks. What he tried to pass on to me was oral history about the struggles that many sharecropper families endured. Billie Griffin's memoir bridged the great divide between oral and written history.

The amazing truth is that Billie Griffin experienced this way of life not very long ago. Even as a child growing up in Chickasha,

---

1   *The WPA Oklahoma Slave Narratives* edited by T. Lindsay Baler and Julie P. Baker, University Of Oklahoma Press, 1996.

Oklahoma, I remember Lincoln School, the segregated separate school for African Americans, allowing time out for the harvest season of picking cotton. It just seemed normal to many families as a means of supplementing other income, but not so for the sharecropper. It was a way of life that meant autonomy, self-reliance, and a quest of circumstance unlike anything that we can imagine. The farmers depended on them, and the sharecroppers depended on God to deliver a bountiful crop. Billie Griffin's account describes that delicate balance, and to my surprise, racial hatred seemed to have played only a secondary role. Most importantly this is a glimpse into a family that lives and thrives today, all because of a migrant sharecropper named Billie Griffin.

Bruce T. Fisher
Curator of African American History
Oklahoma Historical Society

Preface

Billie G. Griffin—I called him Mr. Griffin—was an intriguing storyteller. So much so that there were occasions when I had the most difficult time distinguishing which parts of his stories were true and which were creatively engineered to sound like the truth. For example, Mr. Griffin told me he accepted Christ at an early age but was never baptized. He claimed the day he—among others, I supposed—was to be dipped in the water, to his dismay, the river was dry. They went down to the river and, "Damnedest thing, the river did not have a drop of water in it." And Mr. Griffin never bothered to go back again for the immersion.

Hearing that story and the sincerity with which he told it against a backdrop of his many tales that brought laughter, joy, and human understanding to our lives, we merely stored the "baptismal that never occurred" among Mr. Griffin's other tales in our memory bank. On Father's Day, 1984, at Fifth Street Missionary Baptist Church, Rev. James O. Bradford* extended a call to the altar. Mr. Griffin, who was sitting between Patrick, his sixth son, and me, moved toward the altar and stayed for the invitation.

At the appropriate time, Rev. Bradford asked those who had come forward to give their lives to God if they had remarks. Mr. Griffin did. He retold the story I had heard many times. He had given his life to God a long time ago but had never been baptized, because the river was dry. The eighty-five-year-old, silver-headed giant of a man in a small frame stood tall and said, "I figure there is plenty of water today in the baptismal pool. I am here to be baptized." The congregation stood. Rev. Bradford did not want to delay Mr. Griffin's baptismal until the first Sunday. Instead he arranged to baptize him on June 24, 1984, the Sunday following Father's Day.

Enduring Years: A Migrant Cotton Picker's Memoir is a compilation of the many stories Mr. Griffin told about his life as a survivor during tough times. In editing his handwritten manuscript, minor emendations were made. I let each narrative flow as if Mr. Griffin were sitting next to me, sharing each vivid account in his rustic style, giving a glimpse of those years long gone. Left intact is the power of his rich chronicles that depict struggles, cause tears and laughter, and expose a time that was.

An excerpt from Mr. Griffin's manuscript—entitled "Enduring Years"—was published in the spring 1982 issue of *Westview*. Featured in the journal is a handsome photograph of the storyteller in his bib overalls and his signature fedora slightly tilted to the side. Later Mr. Griffin entrusted his manuscript to me to one day edit and publish.

Billie George Griffin's sunrise was in Cass County, Texas, September 20 in the year 1898.

Billie George Griffin's sunset was in Weatherford, Oklahoma, September 14 in the year 1987.

In between were enduring years.

Gloria Griffin, EdD

*Deceased, August 19, 2013, at the age of ninety-one.

Acknowledgments

Enduring Years: A Migrant Cotton Picker's Memoir was in the incubator for more than twenty-five years. It was with the encouragement and support of Thomas E. Hartwell that it became a quest. I thank him for making sure I stayed the course and for being the sounding board while this project was under construction.

Special appreciation is given to Patrick Curry, who ventured into the attic to locate the manuscript and researched the family files when I needed additional information. It was his and Laina Davidson's suggestion that I provide for their generation a sense of current events in the world, the United States, and Oklahoma during the decades of *Enduring Years: A Migrant Cotton Picker's Memoir*. Laina also availed her journalist skills to proofing and critiquing several of the many drafts. It is my prayer that future generations will read the cotton picker's memoir with an appreciation for unsung individuals with quiet hopes. Our resounding expectation is that they will be challenged to become the promise of tomorrow.

Malcolm Griffin, Sue Griffin, Vincent Griffin, and Adrianne Griffin offered valuable nuggets that further validated the content of the manuscript and confirmed there is glory in tribulation. I treasure you as brothers and sisters.

I became a part of the Griffin clan because Patrick Griffin acted on the sage advice of his father and married me. In memoriam, as in life, I am grateful to Griffin for our bond of love, devotion, and friendship.

Enduring Years: A Migrant Cotton Picker's Memoir is dedicated to Gwendolyn and Tina. You embody the strength, perseverance, and tenacity of Mr. Griffin. You hold the legacy; you are Griffin.

Introduction

The past is a foreign country; they do things differently there.

—L. P. Hartley, *The Go-Between,* 1953

To some Americans the Great Depression began with the stock market crash in 1929, to American farmers the depression began with the collapsing of agricultural prices in 1920, and to many African Americans it began in the bowels of slave ships in the eighteenth century.

Eli Whitney's invention of the cotton gin in 1793 created a need for more laborers, more slaves, more oppression—more depression. This invention revolutionized the cotton industry by increasing the quantity of cotton that could be processed economically. The rapid expansion of the cotton industry during the eighteenth century contributed to the South's strong identity with slavery.

While international slave trade was prohibited by 1808, internal slave trade continued until three significant events occurred: the American Civil War, the issuance of the Emancipation Proclamation, and the adoption of the Thirteenth Amendment to the US Constitution. The American Civil War began in 1861 and is credited with the end of chattel slavery. The Civil War ended in April 1865.

During the Civil War, the Emancipation Proclamation was issued as an executive order and a war measure on January 1, 1863. The Thirteenth Amendment to the US Constitution was passed by Congress on January 31, 1865, and was adopted on December 6, 1865.[2] This was the formal act to abolish slavery in the United States of America, ending oppression for some, but not necessarily ending depression.

Many former slaves remained in the South. They and generations to follow supplied the labor for the cotton industry. Working in the cotton fields was their vocation; in that environment, working in the cotton fields was what was expected of them by others and themselves.[3] Even into the twentieth century, working in the cotton fields was a major means for some African Americans in the South to provide the family livelihood.

The cotton field workers' earnings were not great and depended on various uncontrollable external factors (e.g., the weather, the agricultural market, congressional acts, boll weevils). These

---

2   The Thirteenth Amendment was ratified by the necessary majority of states, twenty-seven of thirty-six states, on December 6, 1865. Four states, Delaware, Kentucky, New Jersey, and Mississippi rejected this amendment. Oregon, California, and Florida ratified the Thirteenth Amendment between December 8 and December 28, 1865. Florida reaffirmed its ratification on June 9, 1868. Two states, Iowa and New Jersey, ratified the amendment in 1866. Texas ratified it on February 18, 1870. It was not until the twentieth century that the three remaining states ratified the amendment: Delaware, February 12, 1901, Kentucky, March 18, 1976, Mississippi, March 16, 1995. The state of Mississippi did not officially notify the United States Archivist of its ratification of the Thirteenth Amendment until 2012, when the ratification was official. "Ratification of Constitutional Amendments," *The U.S. Constitution Online*, 2012, accessed February 17, 2014, http://www.unconstitution.net/constamrat.html.

3   This can be likened to the lifestyle or culture in many coal mining communities during this same period whereby each generation provides laborers for the coal mines. The coal mine owners/operators depend on this pool of individuals to mine the coal, and these laborers believe they are born to be coal miners.

laborers were a part of the landscape in the 1920s, the Depression era. They continued their trade until technological changes in the late 1940s and 1950s modified the cotton industry. Soon mechanical pickers and strippers replaced the sharecroppers and cotton pickers.

Opening the files of his life, migrant cotton picker Billie G. Griffin shares how he and his family endured decades of crushing poverty, discrimination, and segregation in America, the South, and Oklahoma.

GRANDFATHER:
Handing History to the Next Generation

Grandpa were [sic] born in the year of 1823 in the state of Virginia under a slaveholder by the name of Griffin. Later on he were sold to a man in Georgia by the name of Crawford, which he did not like much. Crawford were killed in the State War, and Grandpa were so happy that he danced a jig. So when he were free he were already married and my father [William] were borned [sic]. When Grandpa were set free, Grandpa got away from Crawford just as quick as possible and taken the name of his first owner: Griffin. So he walked from Georgia to Alabama with my dad on his neck.

—Billie Griffin, "Enduring Years," *Westview*, spring 1982

During those first two years after we moved to town, my grandpa came from Texas to live with us. He was my dad's father.

I would go around with him; he used to cut wood for people and cleared up new farmland. He told me all the things that happened in his younger years and what he used to do.

You see, he was a slave up until he was about twenty-five or thirty years old. And the things that he told me that took place and went on in those twenty-five or thirty years would make the hair stand up on your head. Such as the time he gained possession of a *Blue Back Speller*.[4] He was so enthused over learning his alphabets and three-letter words he would shout. In fact, one night, lying down by the fireplace on the floor, he got a little too loud. His boss, owner, or master, as he said he called him, came in the room, took the book, threw it in the fireplace, and burned it up.[5] Well, that was as far as my grandfather was able to get in his education.

Oh, there were so many things he said that went on back there in the early 1800s, such as men even selling their sons and daughters off as slaves. You may know how that would happen, I know. But if you don't know, here is what would occur: The slave owner would see a fair-looking girl about sixteen years old or older, whom he would forcibly make lie down for him, and before you know it he would have a mixed family started. Most times the owner's wife would know what went on. But they were so hypocritical; they would turn their heads to such things.

By the way, that explains why I am one-fourth Caucasian.[6]

---

4   A book first published in 1783 by American educator Noah Webster. During the eighteenth and nineteenth centuries, this foundational textbook was used in schools and homes to teach children to read, spell, and pronounce words. Webster entitled the book *A Grammatical Institute of the English Language*, but it came to be known as *Blue Back Speller* or *Old Blue Back* because of its outer blue hardback cover.

5   Paul D. Escott, "Remembering Slavery: African Americans Talk about Their Personal Experiences of Slavery and Freedom," *Journal of Southern History* 67(4) (2001). Across the South, harsh laws existed that forbade anyone to teach slaves to read or allow slaves to learn to read.

6   Ibid. Slave women and girls were at high risk for rape and sexual abuse. In the South, sexual abuse was a part of the culture that treated black females as property or chattel. The many mixed-race slaves and slave children were evidence that white men had often taken advantage of slave females.

FATHER AND SON:
Rolling Stones

When the old man[7] left us, we moved into the village.
My mother bought an acre of land and she built a house
on it—small three room house; a one and one-half story
affair. We had one room upstairs that was plenty of room
for us as there was only herself [sic] and my brother.

My youngest sister was there and attended a business school until
she was able to get a teacher's diploma. You know in those days
you could start teaching school after you mastered the eighth
grade.[8] She taught school for two years and helped us out quite a
bit until she got married. We farmed a little the next year until
we moved to a very good town where we could get work to do.

—Billie Griffin

---

7   In the context of these notes, it is believed that the "old man" is Mr.
Griffin's father, William.

8   In 1910, examinations by local officials for teaching certificates were
replaced in most states by examinations conducted by state boards or state
departments of education. Normal school was the chief institution to train
teachers for America's elementary schools. These schools offered a two-year
course to students who usually had little more than an elementary education
or two years of high school. Gale Cengage, "Overview," *American Decades:
1910–1919*, ed. Vincent Tompkins, vol. 2 (1996), accessed Nov 8, 2013, http://
www.enotes.com/topics/1910-education/summary#summary-overview.

Circa 1915

Striking out on my own, I worked for different people chopping cotton and plowing. I moved into a one-room shack with no floor, no windows, and one door. I borrowed a neighbor's wagon and team. I hauled me some good clay and spread it over the surface of the ground, smoothed it out, and it became as hard as concrete. I think I lived there about a month or so doing a little farm work, cutting a little firewood for other people.

I never will forget a little incident that happened as I was making some firewood for a man. I cut down a big oak tree by the side of a little creek. That tree was about thirty or thirty-six inches in diameter. I was working on that wood one morning; I had made about four ricks. You know a rick of wood is four feet high and eight feet long, run about fourteen to twenty inches long to the stick. So I was cutting away when I heard a noise in the little creek. I went to investigate. I found some catfish about twelve to fourteen inches long swimming up the creek. That was the first time I had seen water run upstream.

I went back to where I was working, and by the time I got my tools up on high ground, the water was up to the ricks of wood. As I stood watching the water, it continued to rise and flow up the creek. It took that rick that was close to the creek, and the wood began to float up the creek as well. Before I left, I witnessed all the wood I had cut float right off up the creek.

Circa 1920

At this one place I only stayed one-half day and left. Then I went over to a town by the name of Charleston, Mississippi.[9] It was the

9   Charleston, Mississippi, is a city in north central Mississippi that has a total area of 1.4 square miles. It is 79 miles south of Memphis, Tennessee.

county seat of Mississippi[10] County. Believe me when I tell you everybody in that town was from the state of Mississippi. They raised cotton down there! About twenty or thirty thousand acres were planted in cotton.

Now, if you know anything about cotton planting, why, you know you have to plant it in rows; sometimes the rows are half a mile long. It is planted with a planter; sometimes it is a two-row planter, and I have seen some four-row planters. The rows of cotton are about thirty-two to forty inches apart.

The cotton is ready to chop when it is up about three to four inches high. Now, chopping is using a garden hoe about six or eight inches wide to cut up the weeds and leave one or two cotton plants to the hill. That is, you have one or two plants right together at twelve- or twenty-inch intervals. You have to cut the grass and weed between the cotton plants.

Some of those farmers would have as much as one hundred acres in one field. Quite naturally they would get eight to ten—or sometimes there would be as many as twenty—people in the field. Each worker would have to chop one of those rows from one end of the field to the other. Remember, sometimes the rows would be one-half of a mile long!

The farmer would always find some man he knew to lead the

According to United States Census Bureau data, the African American population in Mississippi has varied slightly during the decades. In 2010 the racial makeup of the city was 39 percent Caucasian, 60 percent African American; this mirrors closely the demographics in the 1920s. "American Fact Finder," United States Census Bureau (2010), accessed August 1, 2013, http://factfinder2.census.gov/faces/nav/jsf/pages/index.xhtml.

10   Charleston, Mississippi, is the county seat of Tallahatchie County, not Mississippi County. "American Fact Finder," United States Census Bureau (2010), accessed August 1, 2013, http://factfinder2.census.gov/faces/nav/jsf/pages/index.xhtml.

rest of the gang. They would usually call him the leader, and the others would have to stay up with him, or near as they could. Each worker was expected to chop as many rows as the leader did. A few could not keep up with him, and I was one of them.

Man, all would go pretty good until they started discussing the Bible. Some of the field hands were Baptist, some were Methodist, and some were other denominations. They would get to arguing over the Bible, and this leader would be in the midst of the argument. He thought everybody was wrong but him. If they did not agree with him, the leader would get to chopping faster and faster.

I could not keep up with most of them at the regular pace; you know, I was having a tough time. But it always turns out pretty good. There was this guy named Jessie. He liked me pretty good; he would chop his row and almost half of mine. Boy was I lucky! He would keep me up and get on that leader's heels. That would make the leader slow up.

I sure did thank Jessie. I made it about three or four days and I had had enough. I got my little money and went back to St. Louis.[11]

In St. Louis, there wasn't much going on.[12] I decided to go back

---

11   St. Louis, Missouri, is 370 miles north of Charleston, Mississippi. The city's eastern line is the Mississippi River. The city's total area is 66.2 square miles. It is built primarily on bluffs and terraces that rise one hundred to two hundred feet above the western bank of the Mississippi River in the Midwestern United States, just south of the Missouri–Mississippi confluence. In the 1920s, the St. Louis African American community was stable and relatively concentrated along the riverfront and near the railroads yards. James Neal Primm, *Lion of Valley: St. Louis, Missouri, 1764–1980* (Columbia. MO: Missouri History Press 1998), 410.

12   St. Louis did not escape the Great Depression and its high rate of unemployment.

to Oklahoma.[13] I went to a town by the name of Anadarko.[14] It was in western Oklahoma. Plenty of cotton[15] was planted around there. I ended in Anadarko about the last portion of August 1926. I had a pretty good friend there. He was in the illegal drink business, and I would help him. Every day, the time to pick the cotton was getting closer.

One Monday morning, I got up; the sun was shining nicely.

---

13 Oklahoma is in the Great Plains region of the United States of America. It entered statehood November 16, 1907. In 1920, the population of Oklahoma was 2,028,283. According to the US Census Bureau, in 2011, its population had grown to 3,791,508.

14 Anadarko, Oklahoma, is a city in Caddo County. This county seat is located fifty miles southwest of Oklahoma City, Oklahoma. In 1920 the population was 3,116. Native Americans form a near majority of its population. Agriculture has been Anadarko's economic mainstay. In 1927 the local cotton gins handled over fifty-five thousand bales of cotton and the cotton oil mill crushed nineteen thousand tons of cottonseed. Indian affairs have provided the second major support for its economy. The Bureau of Indian Affairs is located there. Carolyn Riffel and Betty Bell, "Anadarko," *Oklahoma Historical Society's Encyclopedia of Oklahoma History and Culture*, Oklahoma State University, 2007, accessed July 22, 2013, http://digital.library.okstate.edu/encyclopedia/entries/A/A002.html.

15 According to the Oklahoma Historical Society's Encyclopedia of Oklahoma History and Culture, cotton has been a major agricultural commodity in Oklahoma since the arrival of the Five Civilized Tribes and the first planting of cotton by the Choctaw Nation in 1825. The cotton boll weevil arrived in Oklahoma around 1905 and wrought havoc over much of the state into the 1920s; however, cotton farmers continued their expansionist plans. The European demand for cotton drove the price to 34.98 cents per pound in 1919, but the prices tumbled to 9.4 cents per pound, causing the agricultural crisis of 1920–1921. Garry L. Nall, "Cotton," *Oklahoma Historical Society's Encyclopedia of Oklahoma History and Culture*, Oklahoma State University, 2007, accessed July 22, 2013, http://digital.library.okstate.edu/encyclopedia/entries/C/CO066.html.

I learned that they were beginning a little cotton picking and pulling. You know, pulling is pulling the burrs and cotton off together. Picking is picking the white cotton out of the burrs, leaving the burrs on the cotton stalk. You get quite a bit more money for picking cotton than you do for pulling cotton.

Most farmers want you to pick cotton when you first start. It was essential for it to be picked clean, without too many burrs and green leaves; otherwise, the farmers would not get too much for it when they sold it. You were expected to pick it pretty clean. This meant you could not get a lot of cotton too fast. When you gather three or four hundred pounds a day, you are a pretty good cotton picker.

When you start pulling it, some guys get eight hundred to a thousand pounds a day. Of course, they pay more per hundred when you pick it than when you pull it.[16]

I left Anadarko and went out about eight or ten miles west of town to another little town by the name of Fort Cobb, Oklahoma.[17]

---

16 Between 1923 and 1929, cotton became Oklahoma's major cash crop. With the expansion, steps for enhancing production and adopting labor-saving techniques were considered. Some farmers substituted tractors for draft animals in cultivating and planting, and operators in the southwestern counties harvested with a sled, a slotted implement designed to remove the bolls from the stalk when dragged across the field. However, instead of mechanical devices, the technique of snapping or pulling cotton gained popularity. Rather than picking the seed cotton from the burrs, some producers delayed harvest until they could pull the entire bolls from the plant. Although the amount of trash caused higher ginning cost, snapping or pulling cotton had become the prevalent practice by the 1930s. Garry L. Nall, "Cotton," *Oklahoma Historical Society's Encyclopedia of Oklahoma History and Culture*, Oklahoma State University, 2007, accessed July 22, 2013, http://digital.library.okstate.edu/encyclopedia/entries/C/CO066.html.

17 Fort Cobb, Oklahoma, is located in the southwestern portion of

I was thinking about meeting up with the same fellow that I had lived with before; then I found out later that he had left the country. I was lucky enough to see another man that was working about six or seven miles south of town. He carried me home with him. He and his family had begun to pick cotton, so I went to the cotton field with him.

About two or three days later, I ran across another single man out there. On the following Saturday he and I decided to go over to Anadarko. It was a pretty lively town, especially that time of the year. People would drift in from everywhere—Tulsa, Oklahoma City, some from northern Texas. There was lots of cotton in that country.

Farmers would go any place to get hands to pick cotton. Some farmers would have from fifty acres to two or three hundred acres to gather. There were times they would not get it all harvested.

So, as I was speaking to my new pal I met, we decided to go into Anadarko that Saturday morning. We went over, mixed with a lot of people—some we knew and some we didn't. All had one thing in common for the weekend.

We got us a room, and of course, he did his thing and so did I. We enjoyed ourselves until Sunday evening, when he and I got ready to go back to the country.

Caddo County. It has a total area of 0.5 square miles. In 1920 the town's population was 546. L. David Norris, "Fort Cobb," *Oklahoma Historical Society's Encyclopedia of Oklahoma History and Culture*, Oklahoma State University, 2007, accessed July 22, 2013, http://digital.library.okstate.edu/encyclopedia/entries/F/FO029.html.

Ella and Billie (circa 1927).

BILLIE AND ELLA:
Vigilance and Strength

I could meet up with any kind of people and talk to them no matter what kind of people they were or what they discussed because I always read quite a bit. Also, my mother were [sic] a devout woman. She always read the Bible and discussed it with us as we were growing up.

—Billie Griffin, "Enduring Years," Westview, spring 1982

Circa 1926

After tramping around the country for eight or ten years, the thought struck me, *I believe I'll get married and settle down.* You know, just about half all girls or women are about a husband, someone they expect to be with for the remainder of their lives. They want you to have accumulated a little something, have a good job or some good prospects in the future. In my case, I didn't have either. I was just a man; I had pretty good health and that was all.

I had gotten acquainted with a pretty nice girl. She liked me fairly well, but she learned a little too much about me. That is, I had always been restless and a wanderer. As she said, "I'd marry you one day and probably you would be in Mexico, New York, or California the next week." So no deal there!

But nevertheless, I had made up my mind to try and live a married life. I did not give up.

In the next month or two I was out in Oklahoma picking cotton. I spent one weekend in a little town about fifteen miles from where I was living (Anadarko). I had a nice time: bought a drink or two, talked with the ladies, and ate two or three café meals as I was doing my own cooking out in the country where I was picking cotton.

On Sunday evening a friend of mine and I were on our way back to work. We had to ride the train about six or seven miles and then walk another five miles. On our little ride, my friend made an acquaintance with a lady who was on the train with another young lady and an older one. We learned they were going farther west, about fifty miles.

My friend drummed up quite a friendship with the first young lady while we were riding that six or seven miles—so much so that in the middle of the week he influenced me to go with him out where they were living.[18] Now here we were out in western Oklahoma, where we had never been before. We arrived Wednesday evening about four o'clock. It was raining, and that was pretty bad for a cotton picker, if you know what I mean.[19]

---

18   Granite, Oklahoma. Granite is a town in Greer County located in southwestern Oklahoma. It has a total area of 1.6 square miles. Situated at the foot of the Wichita Mountains, it is known for its monument industry, farming, ranching, and Oklahoma State Reformatory (established in 1909). Faye Jo Haynes and Glen E. Burkhalter. "Granite," *Oklahoma Historical Society's Encyclopedia of Oklahoma History and Culture*, Oklahoma State University, 2007, accessed July 22, 2013, http://digital.library.okstate.edu/encyclopedia/entries/G/GR008.html.

19   Inclement weather meant the field workers would not be able to get into the field to pull or pick cotton. If there was no work, there was no pay.

The farmer fixed my friend and me up with a good tent with a floor in it.

But to cap it all off, my friend's young lady had a boyfriend! Lo and behold, the lady told her old boyfriend that she was through with him and left. I had to give up my part of the tent.

In the meantime, the other young lady and the old lady were living in a second tent. There was a one-room shack we used for cooking and eating. I had to move into it for my home.

Everything went along very well for a day or two. Then I began to make eyes and advances toward the other young lady. We discussed life's pros and cons. I stated to her my main purpose was looking for a woman to become my wife. She told me that she had just gotten rid of a fool—that is, another mate—and she did not want to be joined to another.

I told her flat out that she might have gotten rid of a fool all right, but I said to her, "I do not know exactly what I am, but I really know that I am not a fool." I think that kind of turned the tide in my favor. After a few days we were getting along fine; but then along came trouble with a capital *T*.

My friend's young lady's used-to-be boyfriend went back to the city, contacted my girlfriend's fool ("that fool," as she called him), and told him what was going on. He had not given my girlfriend up entirely. "That fool" decided to come out and give us all a big surprise. But it did not work like he had planned.

Just as he was boarding the train to come out our way, which took about seventy-five or eighty miles of travel, one of my friends was at the station. My friend was browsing around and saw him getting on the train. He rushed to the telephone and called the man for whom we were working. He asked him to relay the message to us about what was happening.

The man rushed out to our camp and informed us as to who

19

was on his way out here. We all got ready and went up to a little town that was about two miles distant. I went to the drug store and bought me a newspaper and magazine. So we were all in the car: our foreman, my friend and his girl, my girlfriend, another old lady, and me. We were sitting at the station when the train arrived.

The first person we saw was "that fool" standing on the car vestibule, looking out. To try and make everything look normal and surprised at the same time, my girl rushed up to the train and greeted him. However, he was not in such a pleasant mood. The first thing he wanted to know was where the son of a so-and-so was that she had gotten so crazy about. Of course, she acted surprised and shocked at the statement. She asked him what on earth he was talking about, what he meant. But he would not go for what she said. He pointed me out as the so-and-so.

Here we were, all in one of those little old Model A Fords. My friend and his girl were in the front seat with the foreman. The old lady and my girl were in the backseat, so when he got in, he sat next to the side door on the right. I sat on the left side.

We took off for camp. "That fool" and my girlfriend began to argue and passed a few punches. One thing I can say about her is she stood her ground and was not afraid of him one bit. It seemed as though she had made up her mind that she was through with him completely. Naturally, that gave me more confidence in her and myself.

When we arrived at our camp, he and she went directly to the tent where she and the old lady were living. That old lady was really frightened, as "that fool" did have a firearm. I went and visited with my buddy and his wife. Well, it was not his wife then, but they did marry later and moved to Shawnee.[20]

---

20   Shawnee, Oklahoma, is located in Pottawatomie County, thirty-nine

My girlfriend's former guy stayed out there another two or three days in the cotton patch. I had to work by myself, and boy, I sure did pick cotton hard those two or three days. I would be going fast, but I could still see them both watching me while I was getting that cotton. I would go by them picking twenty miles an hour. And they were watching me get that cotton.

After another argument, they ran together, and when the battle was over, my girl had "that fool" whipped. I took the pistol. Oh, at that time she was much of a woman—weighed about two hundred pounds, five foot five inches, and solid mean!

I stayed to myself in the cook shack. He stayed around, trying to persuade her to go back with him. She refused to go; she said she would never live with him again. She and this man were not legally married, so he went back to Oklahoma City.[21]

After he left, I got real busy courting her. She and I got right down to straight business, and we agreed on one thing: I convinced her I wanted a wife, and she convinced me she wanted

miles east of Oklahoma City, Oklahoma. Its total area is 44.7 square miles. Robert J. Barnard, "Shawnee," *Oklahoma Historical Society's Encyclopedia of Oklahoma History and Culture*, Oklahoma State University, 2007, accessed July 22, 2013, http://digital.library.okstate.edu/encyclopedia/entries/S/SH012.html.

21 Oklahoma City, Oklahoma, is the Oklahoma state capital and county seat of Oklahoma County. It is centrally located within the state. There was significant economic development in the city during the 1920s. Manufacturing firms and automobile dealerships were established. A cotton compress and warehouse was built, and it continued to operate until 1969. The oil industry boomed in the area. Linda D. Wilson, "Oklahoma City," *Oklahoma Historical Society's Encyclopedia of Oklahoma History and Culture*, Oklahoma State University, 2007, accessed July 22, 2013 http://digital.library.okstate.edu/encyclopedia/entries/O/OK025.html.

a husband. And believe me, everything just went fine the rest of our lives.

We stayed out in the country for two more months—two very rainy months. When she, the old lady, my pal, my pal's girlfriend, and I went back to the city, our money was so low that we had to make an arrangement with the conductor for half fare. We arrived in the city and got a room together for about two weeks.

I couldn't find anything to do in Oklahoma City because it was in the wintertime. Work was very slow. However, my girlfriend (Ella, she became my wife later on) was fortunate enough to get a good job at a private home. I moved out close to her, as you might imagine. I was just hanging around, not working. I was not used to someone taking care of me.

Wait! Oh yes, we were in the city for about a month, and we ran into "that fool," her old boyfriend. We had a few hot and salty words. Well, you can understand how those things come about. He made threats and all that. I was in a strange town; didn't know anyone there. So Ella told me to go away and that she would handle him okay. She thought he would probably hurt me, as he was well known there and I wasn't. She had a round with him. It was just fortunate enough that a stranger saw them. He called the police, and they broke it up. We never had any more trouble with "that fool."

Circa 1927

Ella had Thursday evenings off. I would meet her at the bus stop and go down into town, and she would buy groceries for me. We would eat an early dinner and take in a show or visit some of her friends. I didn't feel too well about the ways things were going. I hung around approximately three months.

I had a pretty good friend in Oklahoma City, and he found out that the Santa Fe railroad was building a short line of tracks from Pawhuska, Oklahoma,[22] to another town[23] about thirty-five miles southwest of Pawhuska. He asked me to go with him. I was sure glad, because I was a poor one to let someone take care of me.

I told Ella I was going with him so I could work. She did not want me to go. She thought I just would not come back to Oklahoma City. I promised her that I would come back.

I went to work for the railroad company and saved what little money I could. During this time, Ella and I exchanged letters quite often. I got so excited and carried away after reading the letters

---

22   Pawhuska, Oklahoma, is the county seat of Osage County and the capital of the Osage Nation. Its total area is 3.8 miles. During the Osage oil boom of the 1910s and 1920s, Pawhuska was the site of public lease options. The population in Pawhuska grew to 6,414 by 1920. The Atchison, Topeka and Santa Fe Railroad extended its line from Owen, a community in Washington County, Oklahoma, to Pawhuska in 1923. Pawhuska is 148 miles northeast of Oklahoma City, Oklahoma. Jon D. May, "Pawhuska," *Oklahoma Historical Society's Encyclopedia of Oklahoma History and Culture*, Oklahoma State University, 2007, accessed July 22, 2013, http://digital.library.okstate.edu/encyclopedia/entries/P/PA020.html.

23   Fairfax, Oklahoma. The Atchison, Topeka and Santa Fe Railroad built its railroad from Owen, Oklahoma, to Pawhuska, Oklahoma, and extended it farther to the Osage Junction (Fairfax, Oklahoma). The construction took place during 1923–1927. Carol E. Irons, "Fairfax," *Oklahoma Historical Society's Encyclopedia of Oklahoma History and Culture*, Oklahoma State University, 2007, accessed July 22, 2013, http://digital.library.okstate.edu/encyclopedia/entries/F/FA004.html; Augustus J. Vennedale, "Atchison, Topeka and Santa Fe Railway," *Oklahoma Historical Society's Encyclopedia of Oklahoma History and Culture*, Oklahoma State University, 2007, accessed July 22, 2013, http://digital.library.okstate.edu/encyclopedia/entries/A/AT001.html.

that eventually I quit my job and went on back to where she was. It was on a Thursday.

I arrived back in Oklahoma City about nine that Thursday night. I went down to the courthouse and got our marriage license on Friday. We got married on Saturday, which was the fourth of June in the year of 1927.

On the day before, we had employed a minister to come out there at the time. We got two other housemaids for witnesses. We got married. When the ceremony was over, the preacher went off to cut some lawns; my wife went back to work; and I went downtown on California Avenue, where all the hustlers and gamblers hung out, until late evening. It was just as simple as that.

Of course, I lived out in the maid's house with my wife and began to find odd jobs to do. I can't forget I got acquainted with another man. He had an old Model A Ford. We took the backseat out and knocked the back out to make us a makeshift pickup. We were in business. Well, we worked and got odd jobs around town until the last of August.

I was and always will be a man that loves country life. I was ready to go to the cotton field to pick cotton. My wife liked the country too. She quit her job, and we headed to western Oklahoma.

At first I went out west alone to a town by the name of Carnegie, Oklahoma.[24] It was a great cotton-picking center. I found me a

---

24 Carnegie, Oklahoma, is located on the western edge of Caddo County, almost twenty-seven miles due west of Anadarko. Located midway between Mangum and Chickasha on the Chicago, Rock Island, and Pacific Railway lines, Carnegie boomed in the 1910s and the 1920s as nearby farmers transported their goods, including cotton, wheat, broomcorn, cattle, hogs, and poultry. By the early 1930s, five cotton gins operated in Carnegie. The population grew from 913 citizens in 1920 to its all-time high of 2,063 in 1930. Cynthia Savage, "Carnegie," *Oklahoma Historical Society's Encyclopedia of Oklahoma History and Culture*, Oklahoma State University,

place. As I walked up to this place, I found that there were two or three persons out there from the city, so I did not have any trouble getting a job.

A man gave me the name of a farmer, Mitch Hill.[25] I went out there, and sure enough I got a job. I told him my wife was in the city. He had to go back to the city to get more hands. I went back with him and picked up my wife and our things. Oh, yes, when we got there she was dressed pretty nice. Later on that autumn, Mr. Hill told me he just knew she did not know anything about the country.

And we were back in the country. We were out there a week of Sundays. It was somewhat early for work, so we had seven or eight days to loaf, to rest up, and to wait for the cotton to open up. We went walking around the countryside some two or three times.

On one particular walk we went to see what was called at that time Zolatone Springs,[26] which was about five miles down a hot, dry road. Zolatone Springs were some four or five springs about two or three feet in diameter, just on the base of a small mountain. What was so queer about the springs was that every one was a different color. Some were sulfur colored, dark purple, pink, and green, and one was perfectly clear. Every one had a different taste.

On our way back home, my wife got tired and tried to rest. She got under a little bush about two feet high and tried to get in the shade. Just imagine, she weighed two hundred pounds, and this was a little bush. Oh, we had a big laugh about that.

2007, accessed July 22, 2013, http://digital.library.okstate.edu/encyclopedia/ entries/C/CA057.html.

25   Listed on the 1930 United States Census is a J. Mitch Hill, who was a farmer. He lived in Mountain View, Oklahoma, Kiowa County. Mountain View is eight miles due west of Carnegie.

26   The existence of these springs is a mystery.

FAMILY:
Full House

You have to learn how to hold on to each other in the hard times.

—Iyanla Vanzant

Circa 1927

We did pretty good that fall of 1927. When we started working regularly, we would get paid for whole weeks at one time. We always balanced our books every Saturday noon. The man for whom we were working had a pretty good truck that he hauled cotton in every day. After we got paid on Saturday, he would let us drive the truck into town. There we would cash our check, which was not too much in those days. It was on average twenty to twenty-five dollars each when the weather was good. My wife and I averaged about forty dollars per week. We would buy groceries for the next week, a piece or two of apparel, and, of course, a drink or two of beer or whiskey. We would hang around some two or three hours, meeting other people and learning where the country ball was going to be that night. Then we would go back to camp about five or six o'clock and get ready to go to the country ball.

What is a country ball? It is a dance. For example, you, I, or anyone that had a house with two or three rooms could give a country ball. You would first employ someone with a music box, or maybe two of them; cook something to sell, such as chicken, cake, pies, or chili; and sell other things, such as cigars. Get a man to call figures, and you were in business. There was always a good demand for illegal whiskey. I was in that business.

There were times when we would go back home Saturday evening from town and my wife and I would dress in overalls and jackets. We would put a pint bottle of moonshine in every pocket. We would then start out walking, sometimes as far as fifteen miles; maybe sell two or three bottles on the way. Most times we would be overtaken by someone in an old jalopy who was on their way to the ball, and we would catch on[27] with them. And away we would go!

It was not a big money-making deal. Of course, at that time moonshine was selling for one dollar for one half-pint. We got just enough out of it to take care of our expenses for the weekend and make a little change to get something extra for the table during the next week.

Oh yes! I have to mention something right here that had a great bearing on my wife and me. You see, my wife and I discussed married life between us from time to time, and we talked about what we thought about a family. She told me her story about growing up into womanhood. She said she had gone to two or three different doctors for several months. She said some one or two had told her that certain parts of her body were arranged in such a way that she was hardly likely to become a mother. It was a surprise to me, because a doctor had told me the same thing. It seemed that because of a certain defect that had happened to me, I would never be a father. We laughed about it and forgot all about it.

---

27   Catch a ride.

Circa 1928

One Saturday evening on our way to the dance, the man that drove the truck all the time decided to let me learn to drive. I could drive a little, so I did pretty good all the way. We had mostly hard dirt roads, and sometimes a tricky sand bed would bounce the old truck around if you did not hold sturdy the steering wheel.

My wife was standing up in the truck with several others. I will never forget it. Naturally we had to turn off the main road to come into our place. My wife didn't have enough confidence in my driving, so she thought she had better get out the back of the truck before I got ready to turn.

As she attempted to jump out the back of the truck, she fell halfway out, caught a rod that was on the back of the truck, and finished falling. She was out of the truck for sixty or seventy seconds, but she still held on to the rod. She was dragged ten or fifteen feet before I could slow down. This was after the other people hollered at me to stop.

She was just skinned up a bit, not too bad. We rubbed her up, put on our walking clothes, and started on our walk to the dance. We had to go about ten or fifteen miles. We stayed just until sunup and came on home.

Ella was hobbling a little that Monday morning, but we went on to work just the same.

Watch out! Within two more weeks, she did not have the regular feeling that any other woman would have, she told me. Oh, I just ignored it for another two weeks.

She began to get fussy and a little on the disagreeable side. I remember we were working one day and she had a taste for some ham. We had a little disagreement about it. My point was that it cost too much, that we could not afford it. So from one word to the other, she hauled off and hit me; she partly shoved me over, as I was already leaning. We laughed it off.

The next week, or maybe it was the same week, she decided to go to the doctor. Lo and behold, the thing had really taken place.

Boy, I sure did buy her a ham that next weekend. She cooked us some for breakfast. But the ham "gave out" so quickly that I asked her about it. She told me that each day she had cut her off two or three pieces, put the ham in her pocket, and carried it to the field with her. We got another big laugh. We were always like partners or buddies in everything, and we are even until this very day.

Yes, that's right. She was pregnant. One month after she fell out of the truck, she was pregnant. Of course, neither she nor I had such a thing in mind.

We decided that dragging her behind the truck straightened out her organs. That was all we could lay it to. It was the beginning of my family, namely seven boys and two girls. The first one was a girl. My second child was a boy, born in Mountain View, Oklahoma.[28]

Between the first and last child, there was such a life; many things happened, many things took place. Lots of it seems impossible, but, I will try and tell you about all of the things that occurred in those years—enduring years.

---

28   Mountain View, Oklahoma, is located in Kiowa County, 102 miles west-southwest of Oklahoma City, Oklahoma. Formerly Oakdale, it was renamed Mountain View in 1900, honoring the nearby Wichita Mountains. In 1910, its population was 855; in 2010 the population was 795. Ethel Crisp Taylor, "Mountain View," *Oklahoma Historical Society's Encyclopedia of Oklahoma History and Culture*, Oklahoma State University, 2007, accessed July 22, 2013, http://digital.library.okstate.edu/encyclopedia/entries/M/MO028.html.

Circa 1929

My wife went to Texas to be with her mother when the great event happened. That was in the spring and summer of 1929.

While she was in Texas, we were planning. When I was not working, I would go down on the river and pick me some good willow scrubs about six or eight feet long and one inch in diameter to make me an old-time cradle. I had visited a lady that had a one-year-old child. She gave me the pattern for the length and breadth, which worked out fine. I put it together with nails and glue, sanded it, shellacked it, painted it, and polished it. I wanted it to be all ready when I brought my wife home.

We even had the name picked out—my name, Jr., of course, if a boy. On the twenty-seventh of July 1929, in Waco, Texas,[29] it came out a girl! We used the same initials.

I went down there to bring the firstborn and her mother back home, which was the capital city of Oklahoma. I did pretty well getting down to Dallas, but after I left Dallas on the train, it seemed like the train was going so fast and taking so long I began to feel like it had gotten off on the wrong track. I never dreamed a state was so big.

Finally I arrived at Waco. My mother-in-law, whom I had never met, was up at the station to meet me. I saw her, and she also saw me, but she left without me. I got a taxi and went to the house. When my mother-in-law saw me at her front door, the first thing she said was that she had seen me but had taken me

---

29 Waco, Texas, is the county seat of McLennan, Texas. It is approximately 119 miles south of Dallas, situated between Dallas and Austin. In the 1920s, Waco was among few towns or cities in Texas to institute protection for African Americans and others threatened with mob violence and lynching. Patricia Bernstein, *The First Waco Horror* (College Station, Texas: A&M University Press, 2005), 185–191.

for just a "shave-tail kid,"[30] not her daughter's husband. I took the compliment very well.

I was down there for four or five hours before we started back home. We arrived Monday morning in the city. We rested awhile before I went to work on a shift lasting from 2:00 p.m. until 10:30 p.m.

Well, I had become a family man now. But, as I have stated before, I was a country man; I loved the farming industry. So I worked for about six more weeks in the city and went back to the country to pick cotton.

When we went to the country, about one hundred miles west, we had the truck loaded with so much we had to hang the old-time cradle on the outside. You guessed it; it was torn up by a wreck. Another truck sideswiped us.

There was no one to work that fall but myself. We had to give up our Saturday night outings.

Here is where the test of good times and hard times started, and it continued for the next twenty-five or thirty years. Boy, was it a test!

The farmer I contacted wanted us to stay out all year with him, and we did. I was to have a small amount of money and so many acres of cotton, which was the usual process of the farmers in those days. The person working for a landowner usually worked by the day or month, or the landowner gave him his own field of cotton. So if you didn't have livestock or machinery to do your own farming, the landlord usually furnished these things and you did the labor. In that way you arrived at an agreement. That is called sharecropping, and that was what I agreed to do. He furnished land, mules or horses, seed, and implements. I furnished all the

---

30   Young, inexperienced individual.

labor. At harvest we would split the gross income right down the middle.

We made the deal, and I accepted it. Our trade seemed fair, and it was fair as trades went in those days. I was to do so much work for the consideration of all of the cotton a certain number of acres would make. Of course, you had to depend on all the conditions of nature, including the weather, as there was no irrigation during those years. My wife was to do housework for a little cash. So it seemed a fair trade at the time.

Circa 1930

We moved in the first of the year—1930, to be exact. We hit it off just fine. My wife did some of the housework and some of the cooking; but we got along fine. They were wonderful people. Even today we are real close friends, and that was nearly forty years ago.

But believe me, I had my work cut out back then. I had fourteen young cows to milk two times a day, and some of them were sure wild. Most of them were with their first calf. I averaged about twenty gallons of milk at each milking and had to do it all by hand. I would be milking away on one of those young cows and sometimes I would be almost through with one when she would stomp, kick all of a sudden, and come right down in the pail with her foot. That was milk I had to throw away. This would happen from one to three or four times every day.

That first year I just barely got by. I guess I broke even, counting living, clothes, and a few extra dollars. I planted forty acres of cotton and got forty-two bales, which meant twenty-one bales were mine, about eight cents per pound. Lots of work—not much money!

But here is the surprise of our lives: I guess it was about in the month of March, the year after the girl was born. My wife said she was at the kitchen sink washing dishes and turned around to go toward the cabinet. She said that something felt like it "just jumped" in her stomach; that it almost made her fall to the floor. She hollered to the woman of the house and told her what had taken place.

They called the doctor. He came, and just as you expected, she was with another child. About four months in, and that was the first time she knew it. That was that. There we went with another increase in the family. I had to plan a little differently.

The spring brought us a few showers, and it began to get hot. The summer got a little dryer and a whole lot hotter. By August it was real hot and dry. The increase in the family arrived on the sixth of August: a big boy.[31]

It went on that way until nine had been born. But it wasn't quite that regular; more like eighteen months to three years apart.

By the middle of September, everything in the country had turned brown. My cotton field looked as though someone had scorched it with hot gas. I didn't even need to try and gather it. Now, I didn't know whether I had made a good deal or a bad one, but you know, that is life. You have to take a chance sometimes. I could have very easily made $1,200 or $1,500. I left there owing the man $50 and moved back to the city.

Boy, when I did get back to the city, the panic was on and I was broke. I could only get me one sleeping room and privileges to use the kitchen. That was the year of 1930, and the Depression had set in for real.

I had a friend living in the city that was a good plasterer and cement man. He would get a few jobs and hire me as his helper. I would make about fifty cents per hour with him. That was good wages at that time. Most jobs were thirty-five or forty cents per

---

31   The second child was born in Mountain View, Oklahoma.

hour. Of course, living was cheap. It was a blessing; that it was. Probably we would get about ten or twenty hours' work a month. How I made it I will never know.

Circa 1931

Finally my friend and I went to work the first part of 1931 for fifty cents per hour on the biggest building in town. Sometimes we would put in fourteen or fifteen hours. We did pretty fair. I pinched pennies. I shot a few craps[32] and drank a little, and that suited me. I stayed with this job until autumn.

I rented me a truck and driver in the city and moved out into the country again. It was about eight miles in the country, not too far to go to the nearest town and not too close, where it would be handy for the law enforcement officers to get to you easily.

I got out there about ten days before I was to go to work in the cotton field. The farmer let me have the wagon to go to Carnegie to get my groceries. While I was in town I bought a bunch of bottles (about five or six dozen), a bottle capper, and a small keg (about sixteen gallons) to make homemade beer. We called it Chock; the real name is Choctaw beer.

Some men came after me to play baseball in the country tournament. I loaded up the two kids, and away we went. It was about ten miles away. We stayed out there about four or five days and played baseball. I was a pretty good player in those days. We had a wonderful time out there. Everybody was friendly.

When I did get back to where I was living, my beer was ready. Man, I strained it and bottled it up. I was in business again! After the beer was bottled, I dug me a big hole and watered it down real good; this kept the bottles from busting. On the weekend I would

---

32   A gambling game played with two dice.

Beginnings of a full house (circa 1931).

manage some way to get me fifty or a hundred pounds of ice, and that would keep it real cold. I found a man that was making moonshine whiskey. I went over to his place and got me a couple of gallons to sell by the drink or by the pint along with the beer. Beer was fifty cents per quart; that helped quite a bit.

My wife would cook pies, hamburgers, chili, and so forth for the people to eat when they came to drink and gamble. I carried it all along together. Sandwich for ten cents, beer for ten cents a bottle; I'd take off a nickel or so from the gaming table. We held on to every penny we got hold of.

We had to be pretty close with our little money because another little one was on the way. We had to save every nickel we could. When I started pulling cotton, they were paying thirty-five cents per hundred. I would pull about five hundred or six hundred a day. So you see that wasn't much money.

We had a three-room house, and we sure had a good crowd there one particular Saturday. To be more specific, it was night— about nine thirty—and the date was Halloween. Boy, we had a houseful. My wife called me out of the house. She told me what was happening and said I had to get the house clear.

I went back into the house, and I had a hell of a time getting the men out; they were all men except my sister-in-law. They made all kind of suggestions and excuses, as the poker game had been going good.

Finally I got them out. I had to walk about one mile to the nearest telephone to call the doctor. I was very fortunate to catch him at home. He came right out, and about one in the morning everything was all over. We gave the new addition to the family a nickname that followed him through high school: "Weene-boy" (meaning Halloween).

Well, that was over, and the month was November. We were

gambling again the following Sunday morning. My sister-in-law looked after my wife. We did okay until the cotton began to play out.

Yes, cotton was running out in the fields. The weather was getting cold. Money was really low. I had to go and find me another place to move.

One day in December, about the tenth, I walked nine miles to our little trading town, Carnegie, Oklahoma. It was a one-street western town. All the businesses were along a two- or three-block stretch, at that.

I didn't know what to do. I did not even know what I had gone there to do, but I knew that something had to be done. But what? Just at that moment a man walked up to me and asked me if I would be interested in farming for him in the coming year, not far away. I joyfully agreed and walked back to my place of lodging to announce the good news to Ella. She agreed to go.

After a few days, he came with a four-wheel trailer hooked behind his Model A. We loaded up my meager belongings and had room to spare. We moved about twelve miles south of Carnegie, the same town where I first met this man.

He was a very nice man with a darn good family, three girls and two boys. He had about four hundred acres of land.

Well, I said he wanted me to farm for him, but some people don't understand all phases of farming. As I previously stated, I was in a cotton-growing era. A man that farms much knows getting $900 or $1,000 in those days was doing very well. He gave me twenty acres to work on shares. I did the work, and we split the profit half and half.

I did pretty good in 1932, and he wanted me to stay another year, which I did.

We bought us a used car, a one-seat coupe, that fall. As soon as we got our crops harvested, we took us a Christmas vacation to visit my wife's people for the holidays. We went to Ft. Worth. Our travels went well until I got right over the Trinity River.[33] The old car went to missing and cutting out. I finally made it over the bridge and stopped at the first auto shop. It was nothing too bad. The mechanic fixed it in about twenty minutes.

We went on to my mother-in-law's house. After a very nice time there for three or four days, we returned home.

Circa 1933

In the beginning of the second year, I had another increase in my family. I had to pay the midwife for catching the baby boy. It was on credit, and it was January 1933.

In the spring and summer we carried all the children to the field as my wife learned to plow. The plow was a riding implement. I did all the work with the hoe. I thought I was set up pretty good for another year.

But Mr. Bankhead[34] of Alabama stopped all that. He introduced

---

33 The Trinity River is a 710-mile-long river. It is the longest river that flows entirely within the state of Texas. It rises in extreme north Texas, a few miles south of the Red River. (The Red River is the second-largest river basin in the southern Great Plains. It rises in the Texas Panhandle and flows east, where it acts as the border between Oklahoma and Texas.) The headwaters of the Trinity River are separated by the high bluffs on the south side of the Red River. Wayne Gard, "Trinity River," *Handbook of Texas Online*, Texas State Historical Association, accessed August 8, 2013, http://www.tshaonline.org/handbook/online/articles/rnt02.

34 John H. Bankhead II, US Senator from 1931 to his death in 1946, worked at passage of various pieces of New Deal legislation to benefit cotton farmers. The Subsistence Act of 1933 compensated farmers for leaving land fallow in order to reduce the supply of cotton and to trigger a price increase. The Cotton Control Act of 1934, also known as the Bankhead Cotton

a bill in Congress, and it passed. It paid the farmers as landowners to let so many acres grow up in grass and weeds. Of course they accepted it, greedily. So no more farming for fellows like me! That put thousands of men and families like me right out of anything to do. I had to move out of the little house I was living in and try to get closer to town, where I might find a little something to do.

Circa 1934

In April of that year we had another increase in the family. My wife and I were working in the garden and, of course, that familiar pain hit her. So we both knew what to expect. By the time we walked to the house, which was about three hundred feet away, and got her in the bed, I was not able to leave her and go to the telephone for the doctor. That was the time I took over and became the doctor myself, and I performed excellently. He is one of my healthiest boys, working in the Kansas City, Missouri, post office; he is about thirty-five years old as I write this story.

I was living about four miles from town, and I would go over there and do yard work and so forth. We did very well that year with a little moonshining on the side. I also was living pretty close

Control Act of 1934, controlled cotton production even more tightly. In January 1936 the US Supreme Court dealt a blow to the Bankhead regime when the Agricultural Adjustment Act was declared unconstitutional. Congress repealed the Bankhead Act one month later.

Prior to being elected to the US Senate, Bankhead II was a member of the Alabama House of Representatives. After Alabama's grandfather clause, which disenfranchised most African American voters, Bankhead II was one of the authors of Alabama's revised voting law, which effectively kept most African American voters from registering, through a series of tests and poll taxes. Angela Jill Cooley, "John Hollis Bankhead II," *The Encyclopedia of Alabama,* University of Alabama, November 20, 2011, accessed July 19, 2013, http://www.encyclopediaofalabama.org/face/Article.jsp?id=h1424.

to a plum orchard and would pick plums and sell them for fifty cents a bushel. I thought I would be there another year.

About the middle of October that year, we had the second flood. I was living about three hundred yards from the river at that time. The water got up about four feet in the house. The man I worked for had left me a team of mules and a good wagon for such emergencies. I loaded up just as soon as the water began to cover the yard. About nine in the morning, I just drove up to a hill in the middle of the road and stayed all day and night with my family in the wagon. On the ground we made a big bonfire.

We made it all right. By the second evening, we were able to go back home. We began to clean up. We didn't have too much to clean, as we had left the floors and windows open and the water was pretty swift. When the water dried up, the man who had rented us the place came out and made a deal with me to stay another year. I agreed.

But in the meantime, he had about twelve or fourteen hundred pounds of cotton picked and lying on the ground. During the flood he didn't lose it, but the water had taken the whole stack and lifted it up and floated it off about a hundred yards. It stopped on a little patch of high ground. The water had deposited about five or six hundred pounds of sandy mud with the cotton. He gathered it up and carried it to the gin. Mind you now, the gin was owned by the man that owned the farm, and the owner was not the man for whom I was working.

When he carried it to the gin, it looked white and clean on top, but it contained about five hundred pounds of brownish sand that had settled on the bottom part of the load of cotton. When he had it ginned, he sold it at the prevailing price per pound. After a day or two the gin owner decided to cut a sample out of the bale and sent it off for a test in fiber length, such as 1 1/8 and 7/8 inches in length. When he cut into this particular bale, he found out he had bought about three hundred pounds of cotton and about two hundred or two hundred and fifty pounds of dirt. He did not have anything to sell. That made him quite angry, of course, with this fellow I was working for, and he rejected the lease on the farm.

So there I was, without a place to live, but I had been wise enough to plow me up a garden and plant me some seeds. You see, I knew the day would not be too far away when the owner of the farm would come out to tell me to move, which he did.

I showed him the work I had done, expecting to stay through that year. On top of that, I had my wife go back to bed as though she were sick. He sensed this but could not do a thing about it. So he paid me twenty-five or thirty dollars, which was a great deal of money in those days when you were only getting about seventy-five cents a day for labor. He also promised to move me when I found a place to move. Within two or three days, I finally found a place and he moved me.

Now, right here I want to tell you about the place I found to move to. It was in the next town east, about eight or nine miles from where I was. It was about 1½ miles out in the country with an Indian family.

This house, if you could call it a house, was only one room, about fourteen by fourteen, boarded up with one swing-out window. It had one box door, and about one-third of the roof was gone. I never will forget the first two or three days and night we stayed in it. You could lie down in the bed on your back and pick out any star that you desired: the North Star, the Big and Little Dippers, any of them.

But the most comical thing about it was one morning, about ten or eleven o'clock, my wife was nursing the baby from her breast and singing one of those down-home lullabies, and along came a pigeon flying overhead. Just as it got over the opening in the roof, it had a bowel movement. My wife and the baby had to have a bath from head to foot.

After that I went to town and got me a couple bundles of shingles, and I patched the roof. The Indian lady had a tent she let us have for a dining room and kitchen. We got along fine, considering our circumstances. Of course, the cows pushed the tent down once or twice. I think a storm blew it down too.

We stayed there all the summer until about the middle of autumn. I moved with a barber—that is, he ran a barber shop in a little village and carried on a little farming on the side. I moved onto his farm and went to work for him. Everything went as well as we could expect all through the fall and winter.

Circa 1936

About February the next year, the barber and I made an agreement. I was to carry on his farming. All the work for a thirteen-acre field of cotton was a very fair proposition. In a fair season, that field could have made me about eight or ten bales of cotton, which would have been very good. I had my work cut out for me. I took care of his crops, fixed fences, and milked a couple of cows.

In the spring, we had another addition to our family, another boy. As usual, it happened so suddenly that I had to act as doctor, this time on the second of May.

Well, everything went good until up in the summer. My cotton was looking good, like it might exceed the average. I had between twelve and thirteen acres, and it looked as though I would make a bale per acre. We all were very proud, figuring on the future, of course. But let me tell you, in July there came a crop of grasshoppers.

As the time passed, the grasshoppers increased, and man,

they were sure hungry! Nothing satisfied their appetite but cotton! They ate blooms, squares, and bolls. In about two months I only had a big field of cotton stalks. When the few bolls that were left began to open, I went over the whole field. I got eight hundred pounds. So I quit it. The barber was responsible for my groceries that spring and summer, which was far too much. I had a good chance to work for the other people, so I just owed about ninety dollars.

The barber wanted me to pick cotton and pay the debt. So I solidly told him no. He could just take over the crop, as it was supposed to take care of everything and that was that. But of course, you guessed it, I had to move. I just can't give an account of how I moved or who moved me. I do know that I moved about eighteen to twenty miles due south, to Mountain View, Oklahoma.

I was out in the middle of an eighty-acre pasture on the prairie with about fifteen to twenty-five cows in it. One advantage I did have was that I was living in a good house and was about twenty yards from a good, clear, running creek, with all the wood I needed, as it grew abundantly on the banks of the creek.

I didn't have a job or nothing to do, but I was a fellow that could get acquainted fast. So I went from farmer to farmer in the neighborhood and got to know them. I let them know that I wanted to work and could work. I got jobs from time to time, first one and then another. This was still in the Depression of the 1930s.

When I got hold of thirty or forty dollars per week, I was doing fair. My wife and I would work together, as we never were no more than a fourth of a mile from the house and the children.

However, we were so far from town it was hard for me to get there and back. As good fortune had it, I had a sister living and working in New York City. She sent me a hundred dollars to get me an old secondhand car, and I was in business.

Oh yes! Before I got my car, I got a letter from the state relief board located in the county seat town, which was about thirty-five miles from where I lived. They told me to come over and get me some commodities and sign up for a relief check. It sounded too good to pass up, so I struck out walking.

I got there. But when I did get there, it was too late to go to the office. I had to spend the night in town. That was no trouble; I just got me some two or three newspapers and bedded down in a boxcar. I was up early the next morning, and I was about the first one to arrive at the relief office. They interviewed me and approved me for aid. They allowed me seventeen dollars per month and gave me a big sack of grapefruit and four small boxes of raisins. That was all. I took them and threw them across my back and started on my way back home.

I got two or three rides on my way. The last man went out of his way some four or five miles to carry me to my place about one-fourth of a mile from the house. As it was located out in a big pasture without too many trees, the children could see me as I got out of the car. They saw me with that big sack on my shoulder, about fifty or sixty pounds; they knew I had a great variety of foods.

When I got home, they had a big fire already made in the cook stove. You just can imagine how my wife and I felt as we looked into the eyes of the disappointed children, but we cheered them up by saying that was all they had at the particular time. This was true. They said they would have much more the next time. They had just got the program underway, and it was filled to capacity. Some of the kids could understand this, and it did not matter too much with the younger ones.

Well, all the farmers got to farming and planting seeds for cotton and small grains. I ran out of work, and it got pretty tough with me. Finally I got my little seventeen-dollar check. It helped quite a bit. I think I got two or maybe three of those checks, and they weren't going too far.

Someone told a man about me up in Mountain View. He told the man that I was a pretty good hand. The man came down to talk with me, and of course, I was very glad and pleased with the chance to work every day.

He went back home and got his truck and came back to move me. We moved to his place—that is, one of his places. We might call this place his home place. This was the farm on which he lived. He had other farms that he owned, and some he had leases on. I would say he had about ten farms under his ownership and management. In fact, they were scattered out from one side of the county to the other.

I was given a job of plowing. At that time most farmers had horses, mules, and also tractors to plow with. They used the horses and mules to cultivate and the tractors to break up the ground before planting.

He had about sixteen mares, big mares from Oregon that he worked and bred. Some were five or six years old before they ever had a rope on them. He had a big, tall rawbone fellow to handle them, and he sure knew what to do with them. Sometimes we had to snub them down and throw them down to put harnesses on them, but after you got them harnessed they would be pretty good. He and I would drive four horses apiece on what we called a two-row cultivator, plowing cotton. We had to plow about three hundred acres of cotton. Just as soon as we got over it, we started right back over it. It usually took us about eight or nine days to get over it. We plowed it three different times and were through for the summer.

About the middle of August, I thought I would move back to where I had lived around seven or eight years before. I figured I could get a better place to harvest cotton. So I moved back and got me a place to pick cotton. The people were not doing so well on the farm. It was still in the last of the Depression era, and on top of that the cotton was not very good.

I hustled around and made ends almost meet, but not quite. About the last of the fall, my wife was taken down with pneumonia. She was in bed about three weeks without a doctor. I don't know exactly how I made it, but I never gave up. The old car I bought had played out, so I had to walk everywhere I went. I was about five miles away from my closest town.

When my wife did get up and around, we started our two oldest boys to school. They would have to leave home about six thirty in the morning and walk about two miles to catch the school bus. From there they rode about eight miles to school.

It would be eight or nine at night when they got home, especially if the weather got bad and rainy, as we did not have such things as paved roads. Sometimes the old bus would get stuck and they would have to leave it and go to someone's house, having to stay all night.

Today people raise so much hell about a child riding one or two miles in a modern bus on paved streets.

Circa 1939

Well, as winter passed and it began to warm up, I decided to go to the city, which I did. But it did not happen just like that. I thought there would be no work for men and precious little for women. I walked and hitchhiked to Oklahoma City.

There I knew quite a few people and some pretty good friends. One of them had an old wreck of a car. I got hold of five or six dollars, and we took off to pick up my family. We made it out there and back, which was about one hundred and fifty miles round-trip. We hauled everything that we possessed in the car, including the children, which were five. And on top of that, we had to stay with this friend, who had a three-room house.

I was in town; no job, no nothing. I really had to put a good hustle on, and that is just what I did. I hustled junk, made the refrigerator cars in the early morning. I would get pretty good vegetables, fruit, and ice sometimes. I could sell a little stuff for fifty cents or a dollar. And, man, that was money! I made me a two-wheel cart and went to hustle kindling at night. I'd cut it up and sell it for five or ten cents a bundle. I even had to start gambling again, and even learned my wife to gamble.

We got up enough money and rented us a big room and kitchen. But we still scuffled hard. Some nights we would put the children to bed about ten and hit the streets and make some four or five joints a night. My wife was pretty lucky. We would pick up two or three dollars at each place and walk somewhere else and try our luck.

My wife got a job or two. She would make a couple dollars on each job, and one particular job she had I will never forget. It was at a big Methodist Church. Every Wednesday evening she would go up there about eight at night and clean up and wash the dishes. They had a big church supper every Wednesday, and all the food that was left the ladies would give to her. About ten or ten thirty on those Wednesday nights, we had a bunch of friends, mostly men that were in the same shape that I was in, gather around on our porch and wait until she came home.

She would always come home in a taxi cab with a big number-three tub of food. So along about that time of night, the guys would be there. They would hail sometimes two or three taxis before the right one came along. They would push me aside to get to help my wife out and help carry that tub, as my wife was unable to carry it herself. Oh, that's right, you guessed it, she was pregnant again. On those Wednesday nights there was such a feast and eating you never saw the likes of in your life.

That went on about two months, until the last part of June. The new arrival came on the twenty-seventh. As things would be, it was storming and we were down in a basement. The water got about six inches deep. The doctor had to get barefoot, but we made it okay.

Everything went all right; we had to carry him to the hospital only about two times. I would have to walk and carry him; it was about twelve blocks to the hospital. Sometimes I had taxi fare, which was only fifteen cents. It was so close in our little two rooms. It was very uncomfortable, but we stuck it out until the fall of the year, when the cotton began to open.

I think I would have had a much better life if not for the cotton crops. I got stuck behind them because it was something I liked to do. Sometimes I think it was all right as far as keeping my family together and disciplining them the best we could.

When the time came around that fall, I hitchhiked out in the country, to a place which I was well acquainted with. I got me a house to live in and went to the little town close by. I was also well acquainted with most of the businessmen there. There was a grocery store man there that I became a good friend to. He had a big cattle semitrailer that he hauled cattle in to the stockyards and packing houses for other people. I talked to him, and he agreed to pick me up the next time he had his driver to take cattle to the city, which he did. He came by about ten in the morning in that long trailer (about sixty feet) and loaded me and my family in the truck. He placed us in the front part. You could hardly see us. He had to go by the wholesale house and pick up several different things.

We left town about two in the afternoon. The road was not modern in those days, and by the time he got home and unloaded his supplies and got me out to our house, it was about ten at night. It was pretty nice weather. It was about seventy to seventy-five degrees, and we made it okay. This same grocery man let me have a big supply of groceries on time, and besides that he did not charge me a single dime for bringing me out from the city. So, you see, some of us had pretty good confidence in each other.

I got started picking cotton, making a little cash. I went about two miles into town. They had a good little bakery there, so I got me a good little wooden barrel—about a twenty-five gallon malt keg—for about fifty cents. It had about one gallon of good malt in it, which I drained out and saved. It took malt to make the beer that I was going to make. It takes about one half-gallon of malt to make a keg of the beer that we all knew by the name of Choctaw beer. You may recall we cut the name of it short and called it just plain Chock. We sold this for fifty cents a quart or ten cents a bottle. We had a pretty brief trade through the fall and winter.

We were renting a house from an Indian woman who was very nice, but she had a husband of a different tribe, and he did not have a thing. He was jealous of me and his wife. We would loan her money at times to help him, but he wanted to stop that, so he made her get rid of us. It caught me so quick we did not have any place to go. I had to get anything that I could find.

I got me a piece of a house from another Indian family, friends of mine. It did not have a door in it that you could open and shut. We had to use the window on the south side of the house to go in and out. It had been a three-room house in the beginning. The last people that lived in it cut the floor out of the north room for wood. That was the cold side, and they saved enough of the boards to nail up the door.

I will never forget the census woman coming around to count heads. She asked how she would get into the house. My wife told her that if she could not climb through the window she had to stay out. We had a big laugh about it, and she climbed on in.

At that time there was no such thing as a planned welfare program for poor people, and as everything was so cheap, including wages, a family of six or seven could hardly survive. Our locality did not have too many black people living in it. We had a makeshift school for the children and a worn-out station wagon for a school bus. The summer before, they built their first separate school for black children out in the country, about five miles from the nearest village. The people lived in a radius of about forty miles.

One family would be working for one farmer, and another family would be working for another, many about seven or eight miles from the other. We had about eight or ten such families that stretched out in parts of three counties. The little bus would have to make a route of about fifty or sixty miles twice a day. They would end up with about three or four children per day.

Circa 1940

When the weather began to warm up, I began to look for a better place to live. A friend of mine had a farm several miles out from town, and he needed someone to work it. He got me to move out there. We did have a pretty good house to live in. Just a two-room house, but they were very large rooms.

We made it pretty good. I got a chance to work around from one farmer to another. My wife had a chance to work for a minister and his wife at an Indian Mission Church. Maneuvering around that spring and summer, I landed the bus-driving job for the school.

We started school in August, so the children could get out one month—say about the middle of October to about the fifteenth of November—to help farmers harvest the cotton crops. In those days we did not have no machinery to gather the cotton; it all had to be done by hand.

We were living about six miles from the school. It was quite a burden to take care of the school needs. But during the late autumn I secured me a big four-room house about a mile from the school. I got it for a lonely five dollars a month, and I could work out the rent every weekend.

Circa 1941

We were beginning to keep our heads above the water. I had to haul water to the school—drinking water, that is. I would go to town once a month to get things from the superintendent, such as instructions for the school and commodities, all for twenty-five dollars a month. I kept the job one year and a half before I moved out of state.

I moved to Kansas, about twenty-six miles west of Kansas City.[35] Just before I left—well, about the same time I left—there was another increase in the family. I think the boy arrived after I was gone about a week.

I proceeded without my family to Kansas to look the

---

35   Kansas City is the third-largest city in Kansas and the county seat of Wyandotte County. It was one of the nation's one hundred largest cities from 1890 to 1960. It is 351 miles north/northeast of Oklahoma City, Oklahoma. "Population of the 100 Largest Urban Places: 1920," US Bureau of the Census, June 15, 1998, accessed July 19, 2013, http://www.census.gov/population/www/document/twpa0027/tab15.text.

situation over and to straighten the house up for living. It was a very ordinary house for small farm purposes. It was another month before my family arrived, which happened sometime in the month of November.

This was a small place, about forty acres. This was a kind of new deal with me; I was used to three-hundred- to four-hundred-acre farms. I did the best I could, and the reason was that the place belonged to my niece. She was a school marm in the Kansas City School Organization; but in the meantime, she was married to a fool.

Now, you ask me and yourself why I say this. Well, let me describe him this way. In the first place, he had been brought up in Kansas City all of his life. He had never been on a farm in his life, and he was somewhere between thirty-five and forty years old. And another thing, he had gotten used to women taking care of him up to about 85 percent of the time. He did have a job at one time with the hoodlums during the Pendergast regime.[36]

---

36 Tom Pendergast was a power broker in Kansas City's political machine. He maintained this position through influence and association with colleagues and protégés such as Harry Truman and Governor Guy Park. As early as the 1920s, reformers sought to dilute Pendergast's political control. Pendergast was eventually indicted in 1939, resulting in the machine's collapse.

Political corruption did not discriminate in Kansas City. The bars and gambling dens that dotted the city's east side pumped money into that community, but they also pumped more money into the pockets of gangsters and the politicians who controlled them, most of whom were white. "Political Kansas City: Pendergast Prosperity," University of Missouri–Kansas City: UMKC University Libraries, accessed July 19, 2013, http://library/umkc.edu/spec-col/paristoftheplaines/webexhibit/political/pol-06.htm.

"Political Kansas City: The Boss' Buddies," University of Missouri–Kansas City: UMKC University Libraries, accessed July 19, 2013, http://library/

My niece had me come and live out there and look after things for her. When I got there from Oklahoma, I looked the situation over and saw at once that it would be a losing proposition.

On forty acres they had twelve acres of pasture and about twenty acres of land that could be classified as farming land. The house site and barn lot took up the rest. On the pasture they had eight cows, one bull, two horses, and a goat. There were about twelve hogs in and about the barn. And to top it all off, the farm was more like a rock garden than anything else. I did the best I could for about six months.

I broke the land and planted a little corn and about six acres of soybeans, and that was about it, because there were no implements with which to cultivate. I milked the cows, about six of them, to get about three gallons of milk. There were a bunch of cows that were too old and had come from a dairy. They had been on a power milking machine, and they were washed up.

I began to tell my niece the condition of the setup. I tried to tell her the best and the most economical way to make her little farm pay off. But first of all I wanted to know where my living was coming from when the farm was producing about seven dollars a week. At the time, my family had increased to ten, if you include my wife and me, and we were expecting another.

She would relay the information to her husband, and he did not know what end of the cow to get milk from. He told me it was no use of me telling his wife what to do, for she was going to do as he said and nothing else.

I had to get me another job about thirty-five miles from there, coming and going every day. There was no way to go but to walk and try and catch a ride. Of course it was quite a number of people working out there, as it was a big power plant. Sometimes

umkc.edu/spec-col/paristoftheplaines/webexhibit/political/pol-02.htm.

54

I would be on the four-to-twelve shift. Sometimes I had to walk from four to ten miles; it just depended on how lucky I would be to catch a ride.

I did get to use my niece's car, a big 1941 Buick. I got to use it because the tires were getting old and, of course, tires were rationed to workers on defense jobs. You could not get them at once. I suspect her husband put her up to that old trick. The way I talk about him, it will make you think I did not like him. Well, you are thinking just right, because most no one likes a fool, and that is just what he was. Isn't it funny that those kinds of people think everyone is crazy but them?

Well, I got sick and disgusted about the whole setup, and I gave it up completely. I moved out worse off than when I moved in. I got a place about one mile from there and moved. It was just one big room, twenty by twenty, and a basement under it. I had about five acres, which I cultivated. I planted it to garden and for truck patches. I went to Kansas City, got me a job, and went to work. I would come home every week and did pretty well until there was another arrival in the family.

Circa 1944

It was about January. I was living on this little place. I never was a person that liked to be away from my family, and also, my wife's health was failing. She stayed sick most of the time. One day I was talking to one of my neighbors about my family and my wife. He told me that right under the basement there was a big spring, and everybody who lived there any length of time would become sick.

After he told me that, I got real busy as I was working in Kansas City. Why not live there? I took off of my job one day and went money borrowing. It was quite a job. I was new there and not known, but I just put down the real truth. I told the folks what I wanted and what I needed. I had found a place that was for sale. It was not the best place, but it would do.

I was fortunate enough to borrow enough money from two loan companies to pay the down payment. I was in business again! That weekend I went back to the country and told my wife and family. We began moving on Saturday. We finished moving that Sunday, and believe me, it was hard. I did all the moving in my old Plymouth car. My wife was very sick at the time. She barely realized what was really going on, but we made it okay.

This was in the month of July 1944. I had to scheme very wisely, as I had medical bills to pay and get my children ready for school. I had eight kids to make ready for school by September, and by solid thinking I got everything under control.

Circa 1945

After that winter we began to keep our heads above the water. My wife was getting better. She got well enough to go to work again. She went to work at a terminal warehouse.

As the summer closed out, the fall began. I got that old cotton patch fever. So I bought me an old truck, a one-and-a-half-ton job, and headed for the south. I brought five of my boys with me, and we stayed out about ninety days. We did very well. I paid for my truck and almost paid for my house.

We were back in Kansas City. There I went to work on the railroad and my wife went back to the laundry. We really had a hard winter in Kansas City. On the street we lived on, my wife had to walk uphill. Many mornings I had to go with her to push and pull her up the hill because the snow would freeze and turn to ice.

After that winter was over, she began to stay sick quite a lot. I kept plugging along. My boys were beginning to grow into young men. They began to get jobs and work. They mostly worked in the bowling alleys. They did good, helping to buy their clothes and other necessities for school.

Griffin boys take a break with unidentified boys in cotton field (circa 1948).

RESILIENCE:

The Struggle Continues

I have a dream that my four little children will one day
live in a nation where they will not be judged by the color
of their skin but by the content of their character.

—*Martin Luther King Jr.*

Circa 1951

Well, the time of year rolled around again—that is, the fall of the year—and we all began to get that old Oklahoma fever. I got my old truck in good shape, and by the first week in September we took off, of course. That year all the boys were choosing jobs of their own. Some were in high school, and I had one in college in Texas.

That was the year of 1951, and I only brought my two younger boys with me that year. We worked pretty hard in the cotton fields and saved a little money. By the middle of December, my wife decided that she would rather make her home back in Oklahoma on account of her health. The weather back in Kansas City was too bad for her.

I went looking around for a place to settle where there would be a school for my boys to go to. There were just a few towns out in the West that had separate schools, as you may know. This was about the end of the separate-schools era.

So I found a place to move to in a town by the name of Weatherford, Oklahoma.[37] My boys were in the sixth and seventh grades. They went to school for two years in Weatherford until the oldest boy finished the eighth grade.

Circa 1953

Then another headache started. We had a marvelous high school system in Weatherford, but my boy was not light colored enough, so he could not attend. The school system paid his fare on the Greyhound bus to another town[38] fifteen miles away for him to attend ninth-grade classes. He had to get up every morning at five in the morning to catch the bus to ride fifteen miles and had to lie around one and a half hours before school opened.

In the afternoon, after school was out, he had to wait until six o'clock to come home. Does that make sense? Does it really make sense about the American prejudiced school system? Sometimes he would lose so much sleep he would pass by home on the bus as far as thirty-five miles before he would wake up or the bus driver would wake him up. Sometimes I wondered

---

37   Weatherford, Oklahoma is a city in Custer County, Oklahoma. Its population is less than 2 percent African American. It is located ninety miles west of Oklahoma City, Oklahoma; forty miles north-northwest of Carnegie, Oklahoma, and forty miles north of Mountain View, Oklahoma. Vonde Ruchman-McPhearson, "Weatherford," *Oklahoma Historical Society's Encyclopedia of Oklahoma History and Culture*, Oklahoma State University, 2007, accessed July 22, 2013, http://digital.library.okstate.edu/encyclopedia/entries/W/WE002.html.

38   Clinton, Oklahoma.

whether it was his fault or the bus driver was too much of an American dog to wake him up.

So after that school year was over, he said that he didn't think he would go back to school anymore. He declared it was just too much of an effort to try and learn the ways and means of America yet be denied on every count.

The next school year,[39] he was able to go to school in his own town, which he and I were supporting in various ways. He and others were able to finish high school and college at home.[40]

---

39 Brown v Board of Education (1954) is a landmark United States Supreme Court case in which the Court declared state laws establishing separate public schools for African American and Caucasian students unconstitutional. Chief Justice Earl Warren rendered that separate educational facilities are inherently unequal, but the Court did not give directions for implementation of its ruling. Rather, state attorney generals were asked to submit plans for how to proceed with desegregation. After many hearings, on May 31, 1955, the justices handed down a plan for how it was to proceed; desegregation was to proceed with "all deliberate speed." "Brown v Board of Education 1954," National Center for Public Policy Research, accessed July 24, 2013, http://www.nationalcenter.org/htm; "History of Brown v Board of Education," United States Courts, accessed July 23, 2013, http//www.uscourts.gov/educational-resources/get-involved/federal-court-activities/brown-board-of-education-re-enactment/history.aspx.

40 Weatherford, Oklahoma, had one high school; African American students had to attend the all-back school in Clinton, Oklahoma, fifteen miles away. After the May 17, 1954, Brown v Board of Education ruling, Weatherford opened its school to all students the following school year. Vonde Ruchman-McPhearson, "Weatherford," *Oklahoma Historical Society's Encyclopedia of Oklahoma History and Culture*, Oklahoma State University, 2007, accessed July 22, 2013, http://digital.library.okstate.edu/encyclopedia/entries/W/WE002.html.

So this is about all there is to my life. From now on the people of this town and my children can fill anyone in on the other little incidents in my life.[41]

So it be.

Billie G. Griffin

---

41   Mr. Griffin remained in Weatherford, Oklahoma, for seventeen years following the penning of his memoir. He died September 14, 1987. His memorial services were held at Lockstone Funeral Home, Weatherford, Oklahoma. Rev. James O. Bradford, New Covenant Baptist Church, Oklahoma City, Oklahoma, officiated.

Proud parents Billie and Ella stand behind son number six.

Son number six, first African American to play football at Southwestern Oklahoma State University, formerly Southwestern State College, Weatherford, Oklahoma.

Seven sons and daughter surround their father,
Billie Griffin (family reunion, circa 1980)

ENDURANCE:
Glory in Tribulation

*For everything that was written to teach us, so
that through endurance and the encouragement
of the Scripture we might have hope ...*

—Romans 15:4 (NIV)

*Endurance is not just the ability to bear a
hard thing, but to turn it into glory.*

—William Barclay

*And not only [so], but we glory in tribulations also,
knowing that tribulation worketh patience; And
patience, experience; and experience, hope.*

—Romans 5:3–4 (KJV)

Billie and Ella had nine children, all of whom observed their parents'
determination to provide the family livelihood. The nine children
learned solid work ethics and the importance of family unity.

Circa 1929

The firstborn, whose name bears her father's initials, entered civil
service work. She lived and worked in Nebraska until she was

transferred to Clinton-Sherman Air Force Base in Burns Flat, Oklahoma.

Circa 1930

The "big boy" came to be known among his siblings and friends as Flash or Duke. He served a very brief time in the armed services until his age was discovered; he was too young. He returned to Kansas City, where he worked in a bowling alley. He held sundry other jobs, including working in a packing house in Kansas City and Oklahoma City before starting his own tree service business. He attained the Thirty-Second Degree as a Mason/Shriner.

Circa 1931

"Weene-boy" graduated from Sumner High School, Kansas City, Kansas, in 1949. He attended Texas College, a historically black college (HBCU) in Tyler, Texas, on a football scholarship. Upon graduation, he enlisted in the army and served as a clerk at Ft. Leonard Wood in Missouri. He returned to the Lone Star State and taught in Taro, Texas. He later moved to Elk City, Oklahoma. While teaching in western Oklahoma, he obtained his master's degree from Southwestern State College.[42]

He left Elk City to accept a teaching position in Kansas City, Missouri, at St. Augustine High School. His other teaching assignments in the Kansas City Public School District were Douglass Elementary School and Paseo High School. He retired from East High School, Kansas City, Missouri. Throughout his teaching career, he was a football coach. As a teacher, he was a member of the teachers' union, in which he held several leadership positions.

---

42   Southwestern State College was renamed Southwestern Oklahoma State University, Weatherford, Oklahoma.

Circa 1933

The baby caught by the midwife who was paid on credit did what
he could to bring income into the family. When he was about seven
or eight years old, he worked in an Oklahoma City chicken house
and was paid with chicken feet. One day he backed into a stove,
burned his pants, and was unable to work. It so happened that
later that day, a man, in jest, offered to buy his brother. Because he
thought this was a way to make up for not bringing chicken feet
home, he sold brother number five for a dollar. Brother number
five was returned to the parents without incident, and the brothers
laugh about it to this day.

Brother number three entered the armed services after
completing high school. He was an army paratrooper stationed at
Ft. Campbell, Kentucky. Alaska is among the places he completed
jumps. He reenlisted in the air force. He had special duty in
boxing and served in France and Germany. He graduated from
the local junior college with an associate degree in therapeutic
recreation. Later he worked in the physiological ward at a hospital
in Leavenworth, Kansas. At the Bonner Springs facility, he was
the only activity director with a degree in therapeutic recreation.
He also worked at a Veterans Health Administration hospital. He
has a great love for the outdoors and is an accomplished arts and
crafts instructor.

Circa 1934

The fourth son graduated from Sumner High School and was one
of three sons to enlist in the navy. During his four years of naval
service, he and brother number five served on the same ship,
USS *Corsair* 435. A news article was written about these Griffin
brothers as well as a father and son serving on the USS *Corsair*

at the time. The same brothers played one year of high-school football together.

He met his wife in Connecticut and brought her back to Kansas City. While working at the post office, he attended Park College, majoring in business. He answered the call for more air traffic controllers and journeyed to the Federal Aviation Administration Center located in Oklahoma City for collegiate air traffic control training. He served as an air traffic controller for several years in Olathe, Kansas.

He returned to Kansas City and completed his master's in business administration. He retired as a US Civil Service purchasing agent in Michigan as a general schedule (GS) 15. In Michigan he was involved in politics. He was an independent Republican. He also was an active member of the NAACP and volunteered his service as a claim adjuster. His two sets of male twins are bookends with three girls in between.

Circa 1936

As a child, he was known as "Pennies" because he would keep the pennies others gave him and take them home for the family. He learned very early that each penny counted; twenty-five cents was a lot of money back in those days.

Like his brothers before him, the fifth son graduated from Sumner High School. He received a football scholarship from Emporia State University. He left Emporia after his first year to join the navy. He sailed out of Key West for two years. He and brother number four served on the USS *Corsair* 435 together, just as they had played high-school football together one year at Sumner.

He joined brother number six at Southwestern State College to complete his undergraduate education; for three years they played football together for the Bulldogs. When he left Southwestern, he completed an accredited medical technology program and received American Society of Clinical Pathology (ASCP) certification as a medical technologist.

For a year and a half he worked at the Research Medical Center in Kansas City, Missouri; he was the second African American hired in the laboratory. He worked at St. Anthony's in Oklahoma City, Oklahoma, for a year and half. His employment as a medical technologist at the Veterans Health Administration Hospital, Oklahoma City, Oklahoma, lasted for twenty-eight years. He retired to reside in Campti, Louisiana, and to enjoy a life of fishing.

Circa 1939

The son who had to ride to Clinton, Oklahoma, on the Greyhound bus, fifteen miles each way, to attend high school graduated from Weatherford High School (WHS). He was the first African American to play on the WHS football team and was also the first African American to be selected as football homecoming king. He went on to attend Southwestern State College and was the first African American on the Bulldogs' football and track teams.

He was a teacher in the Clinton Public School District and at Lincoln High School in Altus, Oklahoma. While teaching, he completed his master's degree in counseling and was the first African American counselor at Northwest Classen High School in Oklahoma City, Oklahoma. He also served as a counselor at Southeast High School in the Oklahoma City Public School District.

He began his doctorate studies at the University of Oklahoma and completed the required courses for administrative certification. During his long career as a school administrator in the Oklahoma City Public School District, he returned to Northwest Classen

High School and Southeast High School. He later worked at Grant High School and Douglass High School.

In memory of his service to his profession and to students, a memorial scholarship was established in his honor in 2002. Through 2013, twenty graduating seniors were recipients of a Patrick Riley Griffin Memorial Scholarship totaling $20,000.

Circa 1941

The last of the seven sons was born in 1941. He graduated from Weatherford High School and entered the navy. He served in the Vietnam War. When he returned to the United States, he traveled extensively. He was a private driver for celebrities, often delivering their cars to the celebrities' homes when they relocated. He was a talented musician and showman.

Circa 1943

Due to the mother's ill health at the time, the care of the last child, the baby girl, was undertaken by an aunt in St. Louis, Missouri. There she attended Lincoln Grade School and Vashon High School. At the age of seventeen she joined her family in Weatherford and graduated from Weatherford High School. She attended Southwestern State College and participated in the band and choir.

Multitalented and versatile, she excelled in the arts and received additional training in the culinary arts. Her first job was at a funeral home in St. Louis. She was a truck driver for Halliburton for three years before devoting the majority of her career life to health services at Clinton Hospital in Clinton, Oklahoma. She has fun at the casinos and at one time had gone to every casino in Oklahoma.

Encouraged by their parents, all of the siblings endured.

Billie and Ella in their later years,
Weatherford, Oklahoma (circa 1976).

Billie Griffin in front of Weatherford,
Oklahoma, homestead (circa 1974).

References

"American Fact Finder." United States Census Bureau, 2010. Accessed August 1, 2013. http://factfinder2.census.gov/faces/nav/jsf/pages/index.xhtml.

Barnard, Robert J. "Shawnee." *Oklahoma Historical Society's Encyclopedia of Oklahoma History and Culture*. Oklahoma State University. 2007. Accessed July 22, 2013. http://digital.library.okstate.edu/encyclopedia/entries/S/SH012.html.

Bernstein, Patricia. *The First Waco Horror*. College Station, Texas: A&M University Press, 2005. 185–91.

"Brown v Board of Education 1954." The National Center for Public Policy Research. Accessed July 24, 2013. http://www.nationalcenter.org/htm.

Cengage, Gale. "Overview." *American Decades: 1910–1919*. Edited by Vincent Tompkins. Vol. 2. 1996. eNotes.com. Accessed November 8, 2013. http://www.enotes.com/topics/1910-education/summary#summary-overview.

Cooley, Angela Jill. "John Hollis Bankhead II." *The Encyclopedia of Alabama*. University of Alabama, November 30, 2011. Accessed July 19, 2013. http://www.encyclopediaofalabama.org/face/Article.jsp?id=h1424.

Escott, Paul D. "Remembering Slavery: African Americans Talk about Their Personal Experiences of Slavery and Freedom." *Journal of Southern History* 67(4) (2001).

Gard, Wayne. "Trinity River." *Handbook of Texas Online*. Texas State Historical Association. Accessed August 8, 2013. http://www.tshaonline.org/handbook/online/articles/rnt02.

Griffin, Billie G. "Enduring Years." *Westview* (Spring 1982).

Griffin, Billie G. Untitled and unpublished manuscript.

Haynes, Faye Jo, and Glen E. Burkhalter. "Granite." *Oklahoma Historical Society's Encyclopedia of Oklahoma History and Culture*. Oklahoma State University. 2007. Accessed July 22, 2013. http://digital.library.okstate.edu/encyclopedia/entries/G/GR008.html.

"History of Brown v Board of Education." United States Courts. Accessed July 23, 2013. http//www.uscourts.gov/educational-resources/get-involved/federal-court-activities/brown-board-of-education-re-enactment/history.aspx.

Irons, Carol E. "Fairfax." *Oklahoma Historical Society's Encyclopedia of Oklahoma History and Culture*. Oklahoma State University. 2007. Accessed July 22, 2013. http://digital.library.okstate.edu/encyclopedia/entries/F/FA004.html.

May, Jon D. "Pawhuska." *Oklahoma Historical Society's Encyclopedia of Oklahoma History and Culture*. Oklahoma State University. 2007. Accessed July 22, 2013. http://digital.library.okstate.edu/encyclopedia/entries/P/PA020.html.

Nall, Garry L. "Cotton." *Oklahoma Historical Society's Encyclopedia of Oklahoma History and Culture*. Oklahoma State University. 2007. Accessed July 22, 2013. http://digital.library.okstate.edu/encyclopedia/entries/C/CO066.html.

Norris, L. David. "Fort Cobb." *Oklahoma Historical Society's Encyclopedia of Oklahoma History and Culture*. Oklahoma State University. 2007. Accessed July 22, 2013. http://digital.library.okstate.edu/encyclopedia/entries/F/FO029.html.

"Political Kansas City: Pendegast Prosperity." University of Missouri–Kansas City Libraries. Accessed July 19, 2013. http://library/umkc.edu/spec-col/paristoftheplaines/webexhibit/political/pol-06.htm.

"Political Kansas City: The Boss' Buddies." University of Missouri–Kansas City Libraries. Accessed July 19, 2013. http://library/umkc.edu/spec-col/paristoftheplaines/webexhibit/political/pol-02.htm.

"Population of the 100 Largest Urban Places: 1920." US Bureau of the Census, June 15, 1998. Accessed July 19, 2013. http://www.census.gov/population/www/document/twpa0027/tab15.text.

Primm, James Neal. *Lion of Valley: St. Louis, Missouri, 1764–1980.* Columbia, MO: Missouri History Press, 1998. 410.

"Ratification of Constitutional Amendments," *The U.S. Constitution Online,* 2010. Accessed February 17, 2014, http://www.unconstitution.net/constamrat.html.

Riffel, Carolyn, and Betty Bell. "Anadarko." *Oklahoma Historical Society's Encyclopedia of Oklahoma History and Culture.* Oklahoma State University. 2007. Accessed July 22, 2013. http://digital.library.okstate.edu/encyclopedia/entries/A/A002.html.

Ruchman-McPhearson, Vonde. "Weatherford." *Oklahoma Historical Society's Encyclopedia of Oklahoma History and Culture.* Oklahoma State University. 2007. Accessed July 22, 2013. http://digital.library.okstate.edu/encyclopedia/entries/W/WE002.html.

Savage, Cynthia. "Carnegie." *Oklahoma Historical Society's Encyclopedia of Oklahoma History and Culture.* Oklahoma State University. 2007. Accessed July 22, 2013. http://digital.library.okstate.edu/encyclopedia/entries/C/CA057.html.

Taylor, Ethel Crisp. "Mountain View." *Oklahoma Historical Society's Encyclopedia of Oklahoma History and Culture.* Oklahoma State University. 2007. Accessed July 22, 2013. http://digital.library.okstate.edu/encyclopedia/entries/M/MO028.html.

Vennedale, Augustus J. "Atchison, Topeka and Santa Fe Railway."

Oklahoma Historical Society's Encyclopedia of Oklahoma History and Culture. Oklahoma State University. 2007. Accessed July 22, 2013. http://digital.library.okstate.edu/encyclopedia/entries/A/AT001.html.

Vorenberg, Michael. *Final Freedom: The Civil War, the Abolition of Slavery, and the Thirteenth Amendment.* Cambridge, England: Cambridge University Press, 2001.

Wilson, Linda D. "Oklahoma City." *Oklahoma Historical Society's Encyclopedia of Oklahoma History and Culture.* Oklahoma State University. 2007. Accessed July 22, 2013. http://digital.library.okstate.edu/encyclopedia/entries/O/OK025.html.

Dr. Gloria Griffin

About The Author

A native of southwestern Oklahoma, Dr. Gloria Griffin dedicated over 41 years to education. Her academic degrees are BS, MA, and EdD from the University of Oklahoma.

In October 1994, Dr. Griffin became the first female superintendent of Millwood Public Schools, Oklahoma City, Oklahoma. She held this position until her retirement June 30, 2013. During her tenure she was one of no more than three African American superintendents in the state.

She began her teaching career in the Crooked Oak Public School District. In 1974, she was employed by the Oklahoma City Public Schools, where she remained for twenty years. Her assignments in that district included teacher, assistant principal, principal, director of secondary schools, and director of high schools and adult education.

She has many firsts in her life. She is a first-generation college graduate in her family. In 1981, she became the first African American principal at Taft Middle School. She was the first female principal at Rogers Middle School, when she returned to that school in 1983. In 1987, she became the first female director of the middle schools and fifth grade centers in the Oklahoma City Public School District.

Students, staff, and patrons know her not just for her leadership, but also as a role model. As Millwood's leader, she set the stage for thousands of children where the standards are high; the level of performance is high; and the rate of success is high. During her time as superintendent the district was recognized by the Oklahoma

Commission on Children and Youth for its Parent University and received the State Superintendent's Award for quality delivery of career technical education related to School-to-Work. The district was awarded in excess of $3.5 million in external funds, including a School-to-Work grant, a Technology Education grant, a 21st Century Community Learning Centers grant, and two Comprehensive School Reform grants.

Within the church and in the community, Dr. Griffin is most active. She is member of Fifth Street Missionary Baptist Church, where she serves as an usher and a member of the scholarship committee. She has been a past judge for the Miss Black Oklahoma Pageant. She is past president of the Oklahoma City Capitol Rotary Club and past chairperson of the Higher Regents' Oklahoma Minority Teachers Recruitment Center Advisory Board. Currently, she is a member of Oklahoma City North Rotary Club.

A long-time community volunteer, Dr. Griffin was appointed by President George W. Bush to serve on the Oklahoma City National Memorial Trust (2002). She was appointed to lead the Oklahoma City National Memorial Foundation in 2006. She has served the Oklahoma City National Memorial in a volunteer capacity since first working on the committee that wrote the story board for the Memorial Museum in 1998. She is a member of the Memorial Education Committee.

She was appointed to Southwest Education Development Laboratory Board of Directors. She is a past president of that board. She was elected to serve on the National Federation of High Schools Activities Association Board of Directors (2003).

In April 2013, Oklahoma City Mayor Mick Cornett appointed Dr. Griffin to the MAPS 3 Citizens Advisory Board and the

MAPS 3 Citizens Advisory Board's Senior Wellness Centers Subcommittee. She represents Ward 7.

Her many honors include Educator of the Year Award–Women of Color Expo (2013); Distinguished Leadership Award–Leadership Oklahoma City (2008); OASA District 7 Administrator of the Year (2007); Oklahoma African American Hall of Fame (2002); the Oklahoma Human Rights Award (2002); the Leo B. Marsh Award (YMCA Achievers); the Capitol Chamber of Commerce Outstanding Leadership Award and the Delta Legacy: "Women Making A Difference" award at the 42nd Convention of the Delta Sigma Theta Sorority, Inc. (1994).

In addition, Dr. Griffin is a charter member of the Oklahoma Sooner City Alumnae Chapter of Delta Sigma Theta Sorority, Inc.; a member of the Oklahoma City Chapter of the LINKS, Inc. and the National Sorority of Phi Delta Kappa, Inc., Gamma Epsilon Chapter. A member of Leadership OKC Class XVI, she is the first African American to serve as Leadership Oklahoma City adult program co-chair (Class XIX and Class XX).

Her publications include "Linking Superintendent Behavior to Schools Effectiveness," in the *Journal of School Leadership* and "Shadow Discipline: An Option," in the *Oklahoma Middle Level Education Association Journal*. She has made presentations at local, state and national educational conferences. Dr. Griffin is the twelfth lecturer in Ira D. Hall, Sr., Endowed Lecture Series at Langston University.

Her hobbies include gardening, bird watching, and fishing. It is said that overseeing the intellectual maturation of young people is Dr. Griffin's vocation. Sustaining the cyclical growth of polychromatic flora is Gloria's avocation. In the garden, in the schools, in the community Dr. Gloria Griffin leaves her handprints.